# ANIMALS *in* DANGER

# Mountain Gorilla

Rod Theodorou

Heinemann Library
Chicago, Illinois

Designed by Ron Kamen
Illustrations by Dewi Morris/Robert Sydenham
Originated by Ambassador Litho
Printed by South China Printing in Hong Kong / China
05 04 03 02 01
10 9 8 7 6 5 4 3 2

**Library of Congress Cataloging-in-Publication Data·**

Theodorou, Rod.
        Mountain gorilla / Rod Theodorou.
                p. cm. – (Animals in danger)
        Includes bibliographical references (p. ).
        Summary: Describes the habitat, behavior, and endangered status of gorillas
and suggests ways to help save them from extinction.
            ISBN 1-57572-266-6 (library)
            1. Gorilla—Juvenile literature.  2. Endangered species—Juvenile literature. [1. Gorilla.
2. Endangered species.]  I. Title.

QL737.P96 T54  2000

599.884—dc21                                                                                      00-024324

Acknowledgments
The author and publishers are grateful to the following for permission to reproduce copyright
material:Ardea London/ Adrian Warren, p. 26; FLPA, p. 24, FLPA/ Gerard Lacz, p. 4, FLPA/ Fritz Polking,
p. 4, FLPA/ Eichhorn Zingel ,p. 4, FLPA/ Phil Ward, pp. 5, 11, 14; ICCE/ C. & R. Aveling, p. 8; NHPA/
Martin Harvey pp. 13, 17; Oxford Scientific Films/ Richard Packwood, p. 9, Oxford Scientific Films/
Konrad Wolthe, pp. 12, 18, 21, Oxford Scientific Films/ Andrew Plumptre, pp.15, 16, 22, Oxford
Scientific Films/ M. Austerman p.20; Still Pictures/ John Cancalosi, p. 6, Still Pictures/ Michel Gunther,
pp. 7, 23, Still Pictures/ Arnold Newman, p. 19, Still Pictures/ Francois Pierrel, p. 25, Still Pictures/ Mark
Carwadine , p. 27.

Cover photograph reproduced with permission of NHPA.

Special thanks to Henning Dräger for his comments in the preparation of this book.

Every effort has been made to contact copyright holders of any material reproduced in this book. Any
omissions will be rectified in subsequent printings if notice is given to the publisher.

Some words are shown in bold, **like this.**You can find
out what they mean by looking in the glossary.

# Contents

# Animals in Danger

giant panda

black rhino

Bengal tiger

All over the world, more than 10,000 animal **species** are in danger. Some are in danger because their homes are being destroyed. Many are in danger because people hunt them.

This book is about gorillas and why they are **endangered**. Unless people learn to **protect** them, gorillas will become **extinct**. We will only be able to find out about them in books like this.

# What is a gorilla?

Gorillas are huge **mammals**. There are three different types of gorilla. They are the western lowland, eastern lowland and mountain gorilla.

The largest is the mountain gorilla. It has a blacker face and bushier hair than the other types of gorillas. This a is mountain gorilla.

# What Do Mountain Gorillas Look Like?

Mountain gorillas have long arms and short legs. They have long black hair. **Male** gorillas are twice as large as **female** gorillas.

The biggest and oldest male in a gorilla family is called the silverback. He has gray hairs on his back that look silvery. He is very strong.

# Where Do Mountain Gorillas Live?

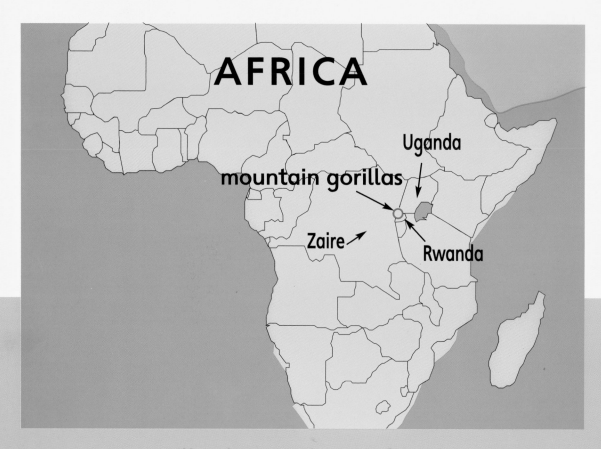

Mountain gorillas live in three African countries called Uganda, Zaire, and Rwanda. They live in misty forests high up in the mountains.

Mountain gorillas spend most of their time living on the ground. They even sleep on the ground. Sometimes they climb trees to find food.

# What Do Mountain Gorillas Eat?

Mountain gorillas are **herbivores**. They eat leaves, fruit, berries, and bamboo shoots. Sometimes they will also eat insects, snails, and slugs.

Mountain gorillas spend half the day feeding or exploring and looking for new places to find food. They spend the rest of the day resting.

# Mountain Gorilla Babies

Gorillas live in groups of about ten. There is always one big silverback **male** who protects the group from **predators**. He stays with his family all the time and **mates** with the **females**.

Females usually have only one baby. It holds on to its mother's chest and drinks her milk. When it gets older it rides on her back.

# Caring for the Baby

Baby gorillas stay close to their mothers for about three or four years. Other **females** take care of the baby while its mother is feeding.

Gorilla babies grow very quickly. There are usually several babies in the group at one time. They like to play with each other and have pretend fights.

# Unusual Mountain Gorilla Facts

Mountain gorillas make nests! Every evening they build a nest with grass and leaves. Then they sleep in it. The nest may be on the ground or up in a tree.

If a **predator** comes too close to a gorilla family, the gorillas will try to scare it away. They stand up and beat their chests with their hands.

# How Many Gorillas Are There?

Gorillas are **protected** by **law,** but there are very few of them alive today. There are only 32,000 western gorillas, and fewer than 5,000 eastern gorillas left.

Mountain gorillas are the most **endangered.**
There are only 500 left today. There are no
mountain gorillas in zoos or safari parks.

# Why Is the Gorilla in Danger?

People shoot gorillas and then cut off their heads, hands, and feet to be sold as **trophies**. Some hunters shoot them to eat their meat.

Sometimes gorillas are caught in traps that hunters have set for smaller animals. Even if the gorilla escapes or is released from the trap it may have been hurt, and might die.

Sometimes mother gorillas are shot. Then their babies are sold to zoos. Sometimes the whole gorilla family is killed just so the hunters can steal the babies.

The **habitat** where gorillas live is being cut down and destroyed. The trees are sold for wood, and the land is used for farming.

# How Is the Gorilla Being Helped?

Killing gorillas is now against the **law**. **Conservation** groups such as the World Wildlife Fund (WWF) are working to stop **poaching**. They want to save the gorilla.

Uganda, Zaire, and Rwanda have places where the gorillas are **protected** by guards. Sadly, the poachers still kill many gorillas.

# Mountain Gorilla Fact File

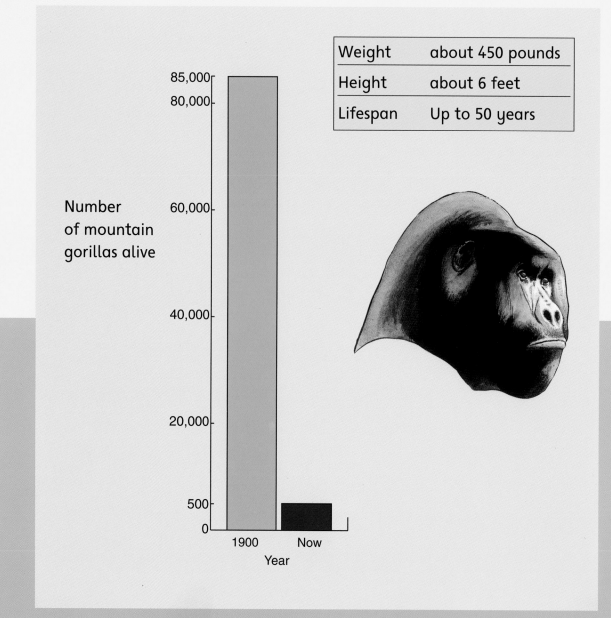

| Weight | about 450 pounds |
| --- | --- |
| Height | about 6 feet |
| Lifespan | Up to 50 years |

Number of mountain gorillas alive

85,000
80,000

60,000

40,000

20,000

500
0

1900    Now

Year

28

# World Danger Table

| | Number that may have been alive 100 years ago | Number that may be alive today |
|---|---|---|
| Giant panda | 65,000 | 650 |
| Bengal tiger | 100,000 | 4,500 |
| Blue whale | 335,000 | 4,000 |
| Black rhino | 1,000,000 | 2,000 |
| Florida manatee | 75,000 | 2,000 |

There are thousands of other animals in the world that are in danger of becoming **extinct**. This table shows some of these animals.

# How Can You Help the Mountain Gorilla?

If you and your friends raise money for the gorillas, you can send it to these groups. They will take the money and use it to pay guards, and to buy food and tools to help save the mountain gorilla.

Defenders of Wildlife
1101 Fourteenth Street, N.W. #1400
Washington, DC 20005

World Wildlife Fund
1250 Twenty-fourth Street, N.W.
P.O. Box 97180
Washington, DC 20037

# More Books to Read

Fichter, George S. *Endangered Animals.* New York, N.Y.: Golden Books
    Publishing Company, 1995.

Kim, Melissa. *The Mountain Gorilla.* Nashville, Tenn.: Hambleton-Hill
    Publishing, inc., 1993.

Martin, Patricia. *Gorillas.* Danbury, Conn.: Children's Press, 2000.

# Glossary

| | |
|---|---|
| **conservation** | looking after things, especially if they are in danger |
| **endangered** | to be in danger of dying out |
| **extinct** | group of animals that has completely died out and can never live again |
| **female** | girl or woman |
| **habitat** | home or place where something lives |
| **herbivore** | animal that eats plants but not meat |
| **law** | rule or something you have to do |
| **male** | boy or man |
| **mammal** | warm-blooded animals, like humans, that feed their young on their mother's milk |
| **mate** | when a male and female come together to make baby animals |
| **poacher/ poaching** | hunters who make money from hunting animals to sell parts of their bodies (poaching) |
| **predator** | animal that hunts and kills other animals |
| **protected** | kept safe |
| **species** | group of living things that are very similar |
| **trophy** | prize |

# Index